Making SPACE
for the SPIRIT

KATHLEEN LONG BOSTROM

Making SPACE *for the* SPIRIT

100 Simple Ways to Nurture Your Soul

WJK WESTMINSTER
JOHN KNOX PRESS
LOUISVILLE • KENTUCKY

First edition
Published by Westminster John Knox Press
Louisville, Kentucky

10 11 12 13 14 15 16 17 18 19—10 9 8 7 6 5 4 3 2 1

Book design by Drew Stevens
Cover design by designpointinc.com
Cover illustration: istockphoto.com

Library of Congress Cataloging-in-Publication Data

Bostrom, Kathleen Long.
  Making space for the Spirit : 100 simple ways to nurture your soul /
Kathleen Long Bostrom.
    p. cm.
  Includes index.
  ISBN 978-0-664-23462-1 (alk. paper)
  1. Christian life — Miscellanea. 2. Christian women — Religious
life — Miscellanea. I. Title.
  BV4527.B675 2010
  242'.643--dc22
                                                                    2009040189

PRINTED IN THE UNITED STATES OF AMERICA

∞ The paper used in this publication meets the minimum requirements of the
American National Standard for Information Sciences — Permanence of Paper for
Printed Library Materials, ANSI Z39.48-1992.

Westminster John Knox Press advocates the responsible use of our natural
resources. The text paper of this book is made from 30% post-consumer waste.

To Ruth—
Aqui en la lucha!
Love, Kathy

INTRODUCTION

In 2005, Westminster John Knox Press published my book of daily devotions for women, *Finding Calm in the Chaos*. For each week's devotions I included "Spirit Boosters," or "simple ways you can nurture your own faith even as you seek ways to offer a kindness to someone else" (p. xiii). The idea was to provide prompts that encouraged readers to nurture their spirits, both by taking time for themselves and by reaching out to others. In this way we respond to Jesus' commandment to love God and to love our neighbor as ourself.

Since that book was published, it seemed to me that the Spirit Boosters provided such rich material that they deserved a book of their own. *Making Space for the Spirit: 100 Simple Ways to Nurture Your Soul* is that book. The Spirit Boosters from *Finding Calm in the Chaos* each now have their own entry, along with a Bible reading (To Help You Reflect), a quotation to provide further inspiration (Who Says?), and a thought-provoking and relevant comment (Did You Know?) to enhance the rest of the material. A space for jotting notes and reflections is provided, thus making this book a spiritual journal that you can keep as you go.

This book can be used as

1. A daily or weekly devotional, or a year-long devotional (choose two entries each week);
2. A springboard for a weekly or monthly discussion group, Bible study, or Sunday school class;
3. The foundation for a church retreat;
4. An occasional resource for when your soul needs a boost.

Follow the entries in the order in which they are provided, or skip around and find what piques your interest.

Above all, allow yourself time and quiet to reflect on the material provided. Some boosters are more challenging than others. Don't rush through them, but enjoy the time that you are taking to nurture your soul.

May you continue to discover an abundance of blessings on your spiritual journey!

—Kathleen Long Bostrom

SPIRIT BOOSTER #1

God took time each day to stop and celebrate creation. God didn't wait until all the work was done to stop and say, "That's good!" Think of one gift of creation for which you are grateful, and say, "That's good!"

Example: "The sun is shining on the lake this morning. That's good!"

To Help You Reflect

God saw everything that he had made, and indeed, it was very good. And there was evening and there was morning, the sixth day.

Thus the heavens and the earth were finished, and all their multitude. And on the seventh day God finished the work that he had done, and he rested on the seventh day from all the work that he had done. So God blessed the seventh day and hallowed it, because on it God rested from all the work that he had done in creation.

(Gen. 1:31—2:3)

Who Says?

Earth's crammed with heaven
And every common bush afire with God.
—*Elizabeth Barrett Browning, poet*

Did You Know?

The earth rotates toward the east at a rate of about 1,000 miles per hour.

Notes

SPIRIT BOOSTER #2

Write a brief note to someone telling him what you appreciate about him. Or call her on the phone and tell her directly. You can write a note to someone in your immediate family, also—it doesn't have to be a person who lives far away. Sometimes it is the people closest to us who need to know that we value them.

Pray for that person each day this week.

To Help You Reflect

All who are with me send greetings to you. Greet those who love us in the faith.

Grace be with all of you.

(Titus 3:15)

Who Says?

I would rather make mistakes in kindness and compassion than work miracles in unkindness and hardness.

—Mother Teresa, missionary

Did You Know?

Benjamin Franklin was named the first postmaster general under the Continental Congress in 1775 (even before the signing of the Declaration of Independence).

Notes

SPIRIT BOOSTER #3

⌒⌒

Write down three things that you do well. Refer often to this list:

1. _____

2. _____

3. _____

To Help You Reflect

Now there are varieties of gifts, but the same Spirit.
(1 Cor. 12:4)

Who Says?

Humility is nothing else but a true knowledge and awareness of oneself as one really is.
—Anonymous, *The Cloud of Unknowing*

Did You Know?

A child's awareness of self starts to become apparent around the age of one and a half to two years, when characteristics such as embarrassment and pride become more obvious.

⌒ **Notes** ⌒

SPIRIT BOOSTER #4

How can you be a light to others? A kind word, a smile, a listening ear—all these are simple ways to brighten the life of another person, whether friend or stranger. Try to share God's light with someone every day this week.

To Help You Reflect

In the beginning was the Word, and the Word was with God, and the Word was God. He was in the beginning with God. All things came into being through him, and without him not one thing came into being. What has come into being in him was life, and the life was the light of all people. The light shines in the darkness, and the darkness did not overcome it.

(John 1:1–5)

Who Says?

There are two ways of spreading light; to be a candle, or the mirror that reflects it.

—*Edith Newbold Wharton, writer*

Did You Know?

Light travels at the speed of 186,282,397 miles per second (when in a vacuum).

—————————— Notes ——————————

SPIRIT BOOSTER #5

Take time to soak in a hot bubble bath, or take a soothing shower. Place lighted candles on the counters and shelves, throw some rose petals in the bath, and play some quiet, calming music. Restoring and cleansing our outside can be a way of restoring and cleansing our inside.

To Help You Reflect

Create in me a clean heart, O God,
    and put a new and right spirit within me.
Do not cast me away from your presence,
    and do not take your holy spirit from me.
Restore to me the joy of your salvation,
    and sustain in me a willing spirit.
(Ps. 51:10–12)

Who Says?

You have made us for yourself, and our hearts are restless till they find their rest in you.
    —*Augustine of Hippo, theologian and philosopher*

Did You Know?

A healthy human heart pumps the entire volume of the body's blood every minute.

Notes

Holding a grudge, or hanging on to a hurt feeling, can be like a window blind keeping the light of Christ from filtering into our soul. Forgiveness is not easy, but sometimes being able to let go can feel like opening a window and letting the fresh air back in. If you can't face the person directly, practice in a private, quiet place, saying, "I forgive you. I forgive you. I forgive you." It doesn't erase the hurt, but helps let off a bit of steam.

To Help You Reflect

So if anyone is in Christ, there is a new creation: everything old has passed away; see, everything has become new! All this is from God, who reconciled us to himself through Christ, and has given us the ministry of reconciliation; that is, in Christ God was reconciling the world to himself, not counting their trespasses against them, and entrusting the message of reconciliation to us.

(2 Cor. 5:17–19)

Who Says?

People often grudge others what they cannot enjoy themselves. — *Aesop, ancient Greek fabulist*

Did You Know?

Being able to forgive a wrong done to you can even lower your blood pressure and heart rate.

 Notes

SPIRIT BOOSTER #7

It is easy to forget to breathe: pain, stress, worry, all cause us to take shallow breaths and even to hold our breath. Practice deep breathing by placing your hand on your abdomen and breathing in slowly, then slowly breathing out. When you catch yourself in a tense moment, stop, and breathe!

To Help You Reflect

When [Jesus] had said this, he breathed on them and said to them, "Receive the Holy Spirit."

(John 20:22)

Who Says?

Smile, breathe and go slowly.
— *Thich Nhat Hanh, Vietnamese monk, activist, and writer*

Did You Know?

Breathing expels both carbon dioxide and water from the body.

Notes

SPIRIT BOOSTER #8

The next time you get a phone call from a charity wanting you to donate used items, think about how nice it would be for the person on the other end to receive something new instead of used. Buy a new article of clothing and give it away, as a way of representing that you are made new in Christ!

To Help You Reflect
He has told you, O mortal, what is good;
    and what does the LORD require of you
but to do justice, and to love kindness,
    and to walk humbly with your God?
(Micah 6:8)

Who Says?
Lots of people think they are charitable if they give away their old clothes and things they don't want.
    —Myrtle Reed, author, poet, and journalist

Did You Know?
Goodwill Industries began as the outreach idea of a young Methodist pastor, Rev. Edgar Helms, who sought a way to reach out to the poor immigrants in Boston.

Notes

SPIRIT BOOSTER #9

Recall a time when someone blessed you with an act of kindness. How did that feel? Cherish that act of kindness in and of itself without feeling obligated to justify or return it.

To Help You Reflect

As God's chosen ones, holy and beloved, clothe yourselves with compassion, kindness, humility, meekness, and patience.

(Col. 3:12)

Who Says?

The sun makes ice melt; kindness causes misunderstanding, mistrust, and hostility to evaporate.

—*Albert Schweitzer, German-French theologian, philosopher, musician, medical missionary*

Did You Know?

The Random Acts of Kindness Foundation is a 501c3 nonprofit organization, founded in 1995. The foundation is privately funded and does not accept donations, membership dues, or grants. The purpose of the foundation is to promote acts of kindness throughout the world.

Notes

SPIRIT BOOSTER #10

If you regularly support a particular charity, pray each day for that charity and the people it serves. You may wish to investigate information on other worthwhile charities and do the same.

To Help You Reflect

"Give and it will be given to you. A good measure, pressed down, shaken together, running over, will be put into your lap; for the measure you give will be the measure you get back."

(Luke 6:38)

Who Says?

Compassion and justice are companions, not choices.
— *William Sloane Coffin Jr., clergyman and activist*

Did You Know?

Charity Navigator (www.charitynavigator.org) evaluates the financial health of more than 5,400 charities in the United States.

Notes

SPIRIT BOOSTER #11

The Bible passage states clearly that we are to love our neighbors as ourselves. What do you love about yourself? If you find it difficult to think in these terms, remember that since we are created in God's image, there are good qualities to be found in every person!

To Help You Reflect

One of the scribes came near and heard them disputing with one another, and seeing that [Jesus] answered them well, he asked him, "Which commandment is the first of all?" Jesus answered, "The first is, 'Hear, O Israel: the Lord our God, the Lord is one; you shall love the Lord your God with all your heart, and with all your soul, and with all your mind, and with all your strength.' The second is this, 'You shall love your neighbor as yourself.' There is no other commandment greater than these."

(Mark 12:28–31)

Who Says?

The love of neighbor is the only door out of the dungeon of self.

—*George MacDonald, Scottish author and clergyman*

Did You Know?

The Talmud is a collection of Jewish laws and traditions, customs and ethics. Talmud means "instruction."

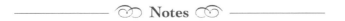

Notes

SPIRIT BOOSTER #12

Find time to compliment your neighbors; tell them how glad you are to have them as neighbors, what a beautiful yard they have, or something similar. Or, do an "invisible good deed," by taking the newspaper to your neighbor's front door, or raking their leaves while they are at work.

To Help You Reflect

If there is among you anyone in need, a member of your community in any of your towns within the land that the LORD your God is giving you, do not be hard-hearted or tight-fisted toward your needy neighbor.

(Deut. 15:7)

Who Says?

If you truly love God, you will love your neighbor. It does not make any difference if he loves you or not.

—*Thomas A. Judge*

Did You Know?

The use of the word "neighborhood" to describe a community of people living in close proximity to one another was first recorded in 1625.

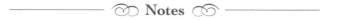 **Notes**

SPIRIT BOOSTER #13

Personalize the following psalm by substituting your name for the pronouns "me" and "I." (Example: "Incline your ear, O Lord, and answer Kathy, for Kathy is poor and needy.")

To Help You Reflect

Incline your ear, O Lord, and answer me,
    for I am poor and needy.
Preserve my life, for I am devoted to you;
    save your servant who trusts in you.
You are my God; be gracious to me, O Lord,
    for to you do I cry all day long.
Gladden the soul of your servant,
    for to you, O Lord, I lift up my soul.

(Ps. 86:1–6)

Who Says?

The first duty of love is to listen.
    —*Paul Tillich, German-American theologian*

Did You Know?

The sense of hearing is mechanical, not chemical, as are the senses of taste, smell, and sight.

Notes

SPIRIT BOOSTER #14

The news is always full of stories of people in crisis. Scan the newspaper or listen to the news and pray for someone you do not know who is in need. As you did in Spirit Booster #13, substitute that person's name wherever you find a pronoun, using the following as a prayer.

To Help You Reflect
In the day of my trouble I call on you,
    for you will answer me.

(Ps. 86:7)

Who Says?
Am I my brother's keeper? No, I am my brother's brother or sister. Human unity is not something we are called upon to create, only to recognize.
    —*William Sloane Coffin Jr., clergyman and activist*

Did You Know?
According to folk etymology, the word "news" is an acronym for "North, East, West, South," although some historians believe the word to be derived from the Middle English word for "new."

Notes

SPIRIT BOOSTER #15

It is helpful to name our fears, so that we can face them and not let them have as much control over us. Name one fear that troubles you, and then offer it to God. Use the image of casting a fishing pole, throwing the fear out into the waters and letting God carry it away.

To Help You Reflect

God is love, and those who abide in love abide in God, and God abides in them. Love has been perfected among us in this: that we may have boldness on the day of judgment, because as he is, so are we in this world. There is no fear in love, but perfect love casts out fear; for fear has to do with punishment, and whoever fears has not reached perfection in love.

(1 John 4:16–18)

Who Says?

Fear imprisons, faith liberates; fear paralyzes, faith empowers; fear disheartens, faith encourages; fear sickens, faith heals; fear makes useless, faith makes serviceable—and, most of all, fear puts hopelessness at the heart of life, while faith rejoices in its God.

—Harry Emerson Fosdick, clergyman

Did You Know?

Theophobia is a fear of gods or religions.

SPIRIT BOOSTER #16

Pray for those who live in fear. Is there someone you know who is afraid? If so, call them or send a note of encouragement.

To Help You Reflect

The Lord is my light and my salvation;
whom shall I fear?
The Lord is the stronghold of my life;
of whom shall I be afraid?

(Ps. 27:1)

Who Says?

Only when we are no longer afraid do we begin to live.

—Dorothy Thompson, journalist

Did You Know?

Fear is a learned, emotional response, but also a basic survival mechanism.

 Notes

SPIRIT BOOSTER #17

Place a small candle next to your alarm clock (if you use one) or on a table or nightstand near your bed to remind you that when you go to sleep, and when you awake, God's commandment is a lamp and a light in your life.

To Help You Reflect

Your word is a lamp to my feet
and a light to my path.
(Ps. 119:105)

Who Says?

Light, even though it passes through pollution, is not polluted.

—Augustine of Hippo, theologian and philosopher

Did You Know?

The ancient Romans are credited with creating the first candles using wicks for people to use to light the way to their homes and to places of worship, and also for travelers out after dark.

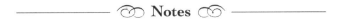

Notes

SPIRIT BOOSTER #18

If you are blessed to have parents who are still living, and who are a loving presence in your life, call and tell them. If you do not have living parents, or if your parents were not a positive influence in your life, call someone who has served as a father or mother figure to you and say how blessed you feel to know that person.

To Help You Reflect
My child, keep your father's commandment,
    and do not forsake your mother's teaching.
Bind them upon your heart always;
    tie them around your neck.
When you walk, they will lead you;
    when you lie down, they will watch over you;
    and when you awake, they will talk with you.
For the commandment is a lamp
    and the teaching a light.

(Prov. 6:20–23a)

Who Says?
The parents exist to teach the child, but also they must learn what the child has to teach them; and the child has a very great deal to teach them.

—Arnold Bennett, British playwright and novelist

Did You Know?
Orthodox Jews wear small, leather boxes called "phylacteries" on their forehead and left arm. The boxes contain specific Scripture verses.

Notes

SPIRIT BOOSTER #19

Is there a particular temptation with which you struggle? Write it on a piece of paper and then shred or burn it while you pray, "Jesus, you know what it is to be tempted. Take this temptation away from me, so that I may worship and serve God. Amen."

To Help You Reflect

Then Jesus was led up by the Spirit into the wilderness to be tempted by the devil. He fasted forty days and forty nights, and afterwards he was famished.

(Matt. 4:1–2)

For details on the temptation and Jesus' response, read Matthew 4:3–10 from your Bible.

For we do not have a high prist who is unable to sympathize with our weaknesses, but we have one who in every respect has been tested as we are, yet without sin.

(Heb. 4:15)

Who Says?

Temptations discover what we are.

—Thomas à Kempis, monk and writer

Did You Know?

The number "forty" is used often in the Bible and indicates a period of testing, ending with a time of restoration.

Notes

SPIRIT BOOSTER #20

The thought of having angels waiting on you is a lovely thought. Do your best to be an "angel" to someone else who needs some extra tender loving care.

To Help You Reflect

Do not neglect to show hospitality to strangers, for by doing that some have entertained angels without knowing it.

(Heb. 13:2)

Then the devil left him, and suddenly angels came and waited on him.

(Matt. 4:11)

Who Says?

Hospitality is one form of worship.

—*Anonymous*

Did You Know?

The Latin word *hospitalitem* means "friendliness to guests," from which the word "hospitality" is derived.

Notes

Thinking back over your life: who or what made you feel protected? Can you relate any of these to images of God? (Example: I always felt protected in my mother's arms. God protects me like my mother's arms.)

To Help You Reflect

For he will command his angels concerning you
    to guard you in all your ways.
On their hands they will bear you up,
    so that you will not dash your foot against a stone.

(Ps. 91:11–12)

Who Says?

At their core, when things really matter, people see a need to turn to God for strength and protection.

—Lee Greenwood, musician

Did You Know?

Psalm 91:14–16 is quoted in both Matthew (4:6) and Luke (4:10) as one of the temptations of Jesus, but Jesus' response is to quote from Deuteronomy (6:16): "Do not put the LORD your God to the test."

Notes

SPIRIT BOOSTER #22

Is there a shelter for abused women in your area? Find out more about it, and pray for those who seek protection there, or who are in abusive relationships but do not know how to find safety.

To Help You Reflect

Let me abide in your tent forever,
　　find refuge under the shelter of your wings.
(Ps. 61:4)

Who Says?

It is in the shelter of each other that the people live.
　　　　　　　　　　　　　　　　　　—Irish proverb

Did You Know?

The word "motel" is a combination of "motor" and "hotel," a concept begun in 1924 to provide ease of travel to people traveling by automobile (still something rather new in that day and age!).

 Notes

SPIRIT BOOSTER #23

Write down a temptation that you have resisted or overcome, and give yourself a pat on the back along with giving thanks to God.

To Help You Reflect

Blessed is anyone who endures temptation. Such a one has stood the test and will receive the crown of life that the Lord has promised to those who love him.

(Jas. 1:12)

Who Says?

Temptation is not meant to make us fail; it is meant to confront us with a situation out of which we emerge stronger than we were.

— William Barclay, Scottish theologian

Did You Know?

There are three kinds of crowns mentioned in the New Testament: the crown of righteousness, the crown of glory, and the crown of life.

Notes

SPIRIT BOOSTER #24

Pray for someone you know who is struggling with temptation.

To Help You Reflect

No one, when tempted, should say, "I am being tempted by God"; for God cannot be tempted by evil and he himself tempts no one.

(Jas. 1:13)

Who Says?

Only those who try to resist temptation know how strong it is.

—C. S. Lewis, British theologian and author

Did You Know?

The word or concept of "temptation" was unknown in many non-Western cultures until the people came into contact with Europeans. In Brazil, Jesuit missionaries translating the Lord's Prayer into the Old Tupi language had to use a Portuguese word (*tentação*), since Old Tupi had no equivalent word.

Notes

SPIRIT BOOSTER #25

Take ten minutes to sit in solitude and be renewed by the presence of God (something that could be done every day, not just once!).

To Help You Reflect

Have you not known? Have you not heard?
The LORD is the everlasting God,
    the Creator of the ends of the earth.
He does not faint or grow weary;
    his understanding is unsearchable.
He gives power to the faint,
    and strengthens the powerless.
Even youths will faint and be weary,
    and the young will fall exhausted;
but those who wait for the LORD shall renew their
      strength,
    they shall mount up with wings like eagles,
they shall run and not be weary,
    they shall walk and not faint.

                                     (Isa. 40:28–31)

Who Says?

There is an eagle in me that wants to soar, and a hippopotamus in me that wants to wallow in the mud.
                     —*Carl Sandburg, poet*

Did You Know?

The wingspan of a golden eagle can stretch to over seven and one-half feet.

——————   Notes   ——————

SPIRIT BOOSTER #26

Waiting can be agonizing, especially if someone is sitting at a doctor's office, or at a medical facility waiting for a test or test results. Offer to sit and wait with a friend. The time will go much more quickly, and your presence can be a reminder of the presence of God.

To Help You Reflect

Wait for the LORD;
> be strong, and let your heart take courage;
> wait for the LORD!

(Ps. 27:14)

Who Says?

Waiting patiently in expectation is the foundation of spiritual life.

—Simone Weil, French philosopher

Did You Know?

The ancient philosophers Plato and Aristotle defined the "Seven Virtues" as an antithesis to the "Seven Deadly Sins." Each virtue has its sinful counterpart. Patience is the opposite of wrath.

Notes

What do you fear? Imagine Jesus touching you on the shoulder and saying, "Do not be afraid."

To Help You Reflect

And he [Jesus] was transfigured before them, and his face shone like the sun, and his clothes became dazzling white. Suddenly there appeared to them Moses and Elijah, talking with him. Then Peter said to Jesus, "Lord, it is good for us to be here; if you wish, I will make three dwellings here, one for you, one for Moses, and one for Elijah." While he was still speaking, suddenly a bright cloud overshadowed them, and from the cloud a voice said, "This is my Son, the Beloved; with him I am well pleased; listen to him!" When the disciples heard this, they fell to the ground and were overcome by fear. But Jesus came and touched them, saying, "Get up and do not be afraid." And when they looked up, they saw no one except Jesus himself alone.

(Matt. 17:2–8)

Who Says?

Change is the nursery of music, joy, life, and eternity.
—*John Donne, English poet and preacher*

Did You Know?

In the New Revised Standard Version of the Bible, there are 539 uses of the words "fear" and "afraid"; and 102 uses of "do not fear" and "do not be afraid."

Notes

SPIRIT BOOSTER #28

Do you have children? Tell them how beloved they are and how much they please you. This applies even if your children are adults. And if you do not have children, "adopt" a neighbor, a child in church, or a friend's grandchild—and tell them the same thing.

To Help You Reflect
While he was still speaking, suddenly a bright cloud overshadowed them, and from the cloud a voice said, "This is my Son, the Beloved; with him I am well pleased; listen to him!"

(Matt. 17:5)

Who Says?
Love does not alter the beloved, it alters itself.
—*Søren Kierkegaard, Danish theologian*

Did You Know?
God's voice is heard calling Jesus his "Beloved Son" both at Jesus' baptism and at the transfiguration.

 Notes

SPIRIT BOOSTER #29

Take a moment to appreciate each of your five senses: taste, touch, sight, smell, and hearing.

To Help You Reflect

I sought the LORD, and he answered me,
    and delivered me from all my fears.
Look to him, and be radiant;
    so your faces shall never be ashamed.
This poor soul cried, and was heard by the LORD,
    and was saved from every trouble.
The angel of the LORD encamps
    around those who fear him, and delivers them.
O taste and see that the LORD is good;
    happy are those who take refuge in him.

(Ps. 34:4–8)

Who Says?

Although we have been taught better, it is easier to assume that nothing that lies beyond the reach of our five senses is entirely real than to acknowledge that what we know about reality through the five senses is roughly the equivalent of what an ant crawling across the front page of the *New York Times* knows about the state of the world.

—*Frederick Buechner, author*

Did You Know?

In order for someone to taste a flavor, the sense of smell must also be present.

 **Notes**

SPIRIT BOOSTER #30

When you're out and about, look people in the eye, smile, say hello—that may be just enough to brighten a stranger's day.

To Help You Reflect

Do not be conformed to this world, but be transformed by the renewing of your minds, so that you may discern what is the will of God—what is good and acceptable and perfect.

(Rom. 12:2)

Who Says?

Almighty God influences us and works in us, through our minds, not without them, or in spite of them.

—*John Henry Newman, Roman Catholic priest and cardinal*

Did You Know?

The term for the study of thought called "noology" comes from the Greek words *nous*, which means "mind," and *logos*, which means "word."

 **Notes**

SPIRIT BOOSTER #31

Society often makes us feel as though we should all be the same. What is a unique quality of yours that you appreciate most?

To Help You Reflect

All these are activated by one and the same Spirit, who allots to each one individually just as the Spirit chooses.

(1 Cor. 12:11)

Who Says?

If I'm going to sing like somebody else, then I don't need to sing at all.

—Billie Holiday, jazz singer

Did You Know?

Human beings are unique from all other species in being the only living creatures that pass on both written and oral language.

 Notes

SPIRIT BOOSTER #32

Affirm another person's uniqueness—and celebrate it together!

To Help You Reflect

I learned both what is secret and what is manifest,
for wisdom, the fashioner of all things, taught me.

There is in her a spirit that is intelligent, holy,
unique, manifold, subtle,
mobile, clear, unpolluted,
distinct, invulnerable, loving the good, keen,
irresistible, beneficent, humane,
steadfast, sure, free from anxiety,
all-powerful, overseeing all,
and penetrating through all spirits
that are intelligent, pure, and altogether subtle.

(Wis. 7:21–23)

Who Says?

Without friends, the world is but a wilderness.

—*Francis Bacon, English philosopher and politician*

Did You Know?

The word "unique" comes from the Latin word *unicus* or *unus*, which means "one."

Notes

SPIRIT BOOSTER #33

Who was (is) an influential person in your life as far as teaching you about faith? Think about the ways that person taught you.

To Help You Reflect

But this is the covenant that I will make with the house of Israel after those days, says the LORD: I will put my law within them, and I will write it on their hearts; and I will be their God, and they shall be my people. No longer shall they teach one another, or say to each other, "Know the LORD," for they shall all know me, from the least of them to the greatest, says the LORD; for I will forgive their iniquity, and remember their sin no more.

(Jer. 31:33–34)

Who Says?

Teaching is a partnership with God. You are not molding iron nor chiseling marble; you are working with the Creator of the universe in shaping human character and determining destiny.

—Ruth Vaughn, author

Did You Know?

The art or science of being a teacher is called "pedagogy."

Notes

SPIRIT BOOSTER #34

For some of us, it is difficult to talk about our faith with others. Think of one way you might share part of your faith story with someone you know. You might tell a story, talk about an author who has influenced you, or share a piece of artwork. As you do this, remember that what you share with another person may help to influence or shape that person's life.

To Help You Reflect

Only fear the LORD, and serve him faithfully with all your heart; for consider what great things he has done for you.

(1 Sam. 12:24)

Who Says?

It is cynicism and fear that freeze life; it is faith that thaws it out, releases it, sets it free.

—*Harry Emerson Fosdick, clergyman*

Did You Know?

A phobia is a type of anxiety disorder. Phobias are irrational fears of things that pose little, if any, actual danger, but these phobias can be quite debilitating.

Notes

SPIRIT BOOSTER #35

Peace begins from within each of us. Close your eyes, breathe slowly, and try to center your spirit in a mode of peacefulness.

To Help You Reflect

"By the tender mercy of our God, the dawn from on high will break upon us, to give light to those who sit in darkness and in the shadow of death, to guide our feet into the way of peace."

(Luke 1:78–79)

Who Says?

Where there is peace, God is.
— *Walt Whitman, poet and essayist*

Did You Know?

Since the Peace Corps began in 1960, nearly two hundred thousand volunteers have served in 139 host countries around the world.

Notes

SPIRIT BOOSTER #36

Is there a situation of conflict in your home, your neighborhood, or your community? Can you offer a peaceful, calming presence in that situation?

To Help You Reflect

"Peace I leave with you; my peace I give to you. I do not give to you as the world gives. Do not let your hearts be troubled, and do not let them be afraid."

(John 14:27)

"Blessed are the peacemakers, for they will be called children of God."

(Matt. 5:9)

Who Says?

What peace can they have who are not at peace with God?

—*Matthew Henry, English clergyman*

Did You Know?

The Guardian Angels, a nonprofit, volunteer organization founded in New York City in 1979, provides education and workshops for schools and businesses as well as patrolling streets, subways, and neighborhoods.

Notes

SPIRIT BOOSTER #37

What is one trait that you dislike most about yourself? God knows all about that, and loves you still.

To Help You Reflect

O LORD, you have searched me and known me.
You know when I sit down and when I rise up;
    you discern my thoughts from far away.
You search out my path and my lying down,
    and are acquainted with all my ways.
Even before a word is on my tongue,
    O LORD, you know it completely.
You hem me in, behind and before,
    and lay your hand upon me.
Such knowledge is too wonderful for me;
    it is so high that I cannot attain it.

(Ps. 139:1–6)

Who Says?

The real fault is to have faults and not try to amend them.

—*Confucius, Chinese philosopher*

Did You Know?

A fault line, in geological terms, is a fracture in a rock in which the rock has shifted apart. An earthquake occurs when there is an energy release caused by slippage along the fault.

Notes

SPIRIT BOOSTER #38

Write down a trait that you dislike in someone else—then tear it up—and try to see that person through God's eyes.

To Help You Reflect

"Do not judge, so that you may not be judged. For with the judgment you make you will be judged, and the measure you give will be the measure you get. Why do you see the speck in your neighbor's eye, but do not notice the log in your own eye? Or how can you say to your neighbor, 'Let me take the speck out of your eye,' while the log is in your own eye? You hypocrite, first take the log out of your own eye, and then you will see clearly to take the speck out of your neighbor's eye."

(Matt. 7:1–5)

Who Says?

Perfection, in a Christian sense, means becoming mature enough to give ourselves to others. Whatever we have, no matter how little it seems, is something that can be shared with those who are poorer.

—Kathleen Norris, author

Did You Know?

The thirteenth-century priest and theologian Thomas Aquinas described the dual nature of perfection as being (1) when something is perfect in and of itself, and (2) when something serves its purpose.

Notes

SPIRIT BOOSTER #39

Identify one hope you have right now. Substitute that hope in the Scripture phrase, "Now faith is the assurance of _____, the conviction of things not seen."

To Help You Reflect

Now faith is the assurance of things hoped for, the conviction of things not seen.

(Heb. 11:1)

Who Says?

We must accept finite disappointment, but we must never lose infinite hope.

—*Martin Luther King Jr., clergyman
and civil rights leader*

Did You Know?

In Greek mythology, when Pandora opened the box that let loose all the evils of the world, hope alone was left in the box. Only when hope was also released did people find a means to cope with the despair caused by all the troubles that assailed the world.

Notes

Identify a hope you have for someone else, something that will make that person's life better; and pray for that person each day this week.

To Help You Reflect

In you, O LORD, I take refuge;
   let me never be put to shame.
In your righteousness deliver me and rescue me;
   incline your ear to me and save me.
Be to me a rock of refuge,
   a strong fortress, to save me,
   for you are my rock and my fortress.
Rescue me, O my God, from the hand of the wicked,
   from the grasp of the unjust and cruel.
For you, O Lord, are my hope,
   my trust, O LORD, from my youth.

(Ps. 71:1–5)

Who Says?

Hope is a waking dream. *—Aristotle, Greek philosopher*

Did You Know?

Project HOPE (Health Opportunities for People Everywhere) began in 1958 with the goal of attaining health care for all, especially children. Their mission statement reads: "To achieve sustainable advances in health care around the world by implementing health education programs and providing humanitarian assistance in areas of need."

 **Notes**

SPIRIT BOOSTER #41

If you live near a body of water—a lake, ocean, stream, river, or pond—spend some quiet time watching the water: how it changes color, how the surface can be still or moving, how it sounds. If you do not live near water, find photos or drawings of water in books or magazines and simply enjoy.

To Help You Reflect

In the beginning when God created the heavens and the earth, the earth was a formless void and darkness covered the face of the deep, while a wind from God swept over the face of the waters.

(Gen. 1:1–2)

Who Says?

It has often occurred to me that a seeker after truth has to be silent.

*—Mahatma Gandhi, Indian political
and spiritual leader*

Did You Know?

About 66 percent of the human body consists of water.

SPIRIT BOOSTER #42

Be aware of the ways you waste water—letting the faucet run while you brush your teeth or rinse dishes; spending a long time in the shower or filling the bathtub full every day; watering outside plants when it is hot and much of the water evaporates. Try to cut back on the waste, remembering that water is a precious resource and, for many people in the world, is scarce and hard to find.

To Help You Reflect

They are like trees
    planted by streams of water,
which yield their fruit in its season,
    and their leaves do not wither.
In all that they do, they prosper.

(Ps. 1:3)

Who Says?

Though inland far we be,
Our souls have sight of that immortal sea
Which brought us hither.

—*William Wordsworth, English poet*

Did You Know?

Shorten your daily shower by just a minute or two and you can save up to 150 gallons of water each month.

Notes

SPIRIT BOOSTER #43

Play some music that soothes your spirit and makes you feel at peace. Do not do anything else but *listen*.

To Help You Reflect

"I have said these things to you while I am still with you. But the Advocate, the Holy Spirit, whom the Father will send in my name, will teach you everything, and remind you of all that I have said to you. Peace I leave with you; my peace I give to you. I do not give to you as the world gives. Do not let your hearts be troubled, and do not let them be afraid."

(John 14:25–27)

Who Says?

Take a music bath once or twice a week for a few seasons. You will find it is to the soul what a water bath is to the body.

—Oliver Wendell Holmes, physician and author

Did You Know?

A orchestra includes four different "families" of musical instruments: strings, woodwinds, percussion, and brass.

 Notes

SPIRIT BOOSTER #44

Some churches have a time of "passing the peace of Christ." Try passing the peace to a family member or friend. Tell that person that you wish for the peace of Christ to be in his/her life, and in your relationship as well.

To Help You Reflect

O God, you are my God, I seek you,
    my soul thirsts for you;
my flesh faints for you,
    as in a dry and weary land where there is no water.
So I have looked upon you in the sanctuary,
    beholding your power and glory.
Because your steadfast love is better than life,
    my lips will praise you.
So I will bless you as long as I live;
    I will lift up my hands and call on your name.
                                        (Ps. 63:1–4)

Who Says?

A great many people are trying to make peace, but that has already been done. God has not left it for us to do; all we have to do is to enter into it.
                    —*Dwight L. Moody, evangelist and publisher*

Did You Know?

Passing the peace of Christ has been a ritual in Christendom for centuries. In the New Testament, the first apostles encourage fellow Christians to "greet one another with a holy kiss" but a handshake or light hug is more common nowadays.

Notes

SPIRIT BOOSTER #45

Count your blessings (name at least ten, but you don't have to stop there). Name them, and give thanks to God, one by one.

To Help You Reflect

Blessed shall you be in the city, and blessed shall you be in the field.

Blessed shall be the fruit of your womb, the fruit of your ground, and the fruit of your livestock, both the increase of your cattle and the issue of your flock.

Blessed shall be your basket and your kneading bowl.

Blessed shall you be when you come in, and blessed shall you be when you go out.

(Deut. 28:3–6)

Who Says?

Scripturally speaking, the spiritual life is simply the increasing vitality and sway of God's Spirit in us. It is a magnificent choreography of the Holy Spirit in the human spirit, moving us toward communion with both Creator and Creation.

—Marjorie Thompson, author

Did You Know?

Practicing gratitude can be good for your health; it cuts back on stress and can even lower blood pressure!

Notes

SPIRIT BOOSTER #46

Think about the people at your church who clean and take care of the sanctuary so that it can be a place of worship, a place to behold God's glory. Use the Scripture passage below as a prayer for those who offer their labors to the church. Call and thank someone, or send a card, saying that you appreciate the work they do that often goes unrecognized.

To Help You Reflect

We always give thanks to God for all of you and mention you in our prayers, constantly remembering before our God and Father your work of faith and labor of love and steadfastness of hope in our Lord Jesus Christ.

(1 Thess. 1:2–3)

Who Says?

Feeling grateful or appreciative of someone or something in your life actually attracts more of the things that you appreciate and value into your life.

—*Christiane Northrup, physician and author*

Did You Know?

Thessalonians may be the oldest Christian document in existence.

Notes

SPIRIT BOOSTER #47

Jealousy and envy create a sense that you are lacking something that you feel you deserve. Be honest about this—if you feel jealous about what someone else has that you do not, why is it so important to you do have whatever this is? Do you really need it? Be aware of any jealous feelings you have and by identifying them, seek to let them go.

To Help You Reflect
Wrath is cruel, anger is overwhelming, but who is able to stand before jealousy?

(Prov. 27:4)

Who Says?
Envy is a denial of providence.
—*Stephen Charnock, English Puritan*
Presbyterian clergyman

Did You Know?
An infant starts to display jealousy at around five months of age.

Notes

SPIRIT BOOSTER #48

If you are jealous of other people's looks, good fortune, or life circumstance, instead of feeling competitive, congratulate them on what it is you admire about them or wish that you had.

To Help You Reflect

If we live by the Spirit, let us also be guided by the Spirit. Let us not become conceited, competing against one another, envying one another.

(Gal. 5:25–26)

Who Says?

Envy shoots at others and wounds itself.

—*English proverb*

Did You Know?

The idea of envy being a green-eyed monster comes from references in Shakespeare's plays *Othello* and *Merchant of Venice*.

Notes

SPIRIT BOOSTER #49

Repeat these words as if God were speaking to you: "Where you go, I will go; where you lodge, I will lodge; your people are my people, and I am your God."

To Help You Reflect

But Ruth said, "Do not press me to leave you or to turn back from following you! Where you go, I will go; where you lodge, I will lodge; your people shall be my people, and your God my God. Where you die, I will die—there will I be buried. May the LORD do thus and so to me, and more as well, if even death parts me from you!"

(Ruth 1:16–17)

Who Says?

Promises are the uniquely human way of ordering the future, making it predictable and reliable to the extent that this is humanly possible.

—*Hannah Arendt, philosopher and political activist*

Did You Know?

Ruth is listed in the genealogy of Jesus (Matt. 1:5).

Notes

SPIRIT BOOSTER #50

Take time this week to look at old photographs of family, and thank God for each person who is part of your life even if you never met.

To Help You Reflect

Long ago God spoke to our ancestors in many and various ways by the prophets, but in these last days he has spoken to us by a Son, whom he appointed heir of all things, through whom he also created the worlds. He is the reflection of God's glory and the exact imprint of God's very being, and he sustains all things by his powerful word.

(Heb. 1:1–3)

Who Says?

It is the creative potential itself in human beings that is the image of God.

—*Mary Daly, philosopher and theologian*

Did You Know?

The first known photograph was taken by the French inventor Joseph-Nicéphore Niepce in 1825.

Notes

SPIRIT BOOSTER #51

Jesus invited all of the disciples to the Last Supper, even though he knew one would betray him. Think about how Jesus invites you to discipleship—no matter what you have done with your life.

To Help You Reflect

When it was evening, [Jesus] came with the twelve. And when they had taken their places and were eating, Jesus said, "Truly I tell you, one of you will betray me, one who is eating with me." They began to be distressed and to say to him one after another, "Surely, not I?" . . .

Peter said to him, "Even though all become deserters, I will not." Jesus said to him, "Truly I tell you, this day, this very night, before the cock crows twice, you will deny me three times." But he said vehemently, "Even though I must die with you, I will not deny you." And all of them said the same.

(Mark 14:17–19, 29–31)

Who Says?

We praise God not to celebrate our own faith but to give thanks for the faith God has in us.

—Kathleen Norris, author

Did You Know?

A disciple is one who takes instruction from a teacher or leader, and is from the same root as the word "discipline."

 Notes

SPIRIT BOOSTER #52

Is there someone who has betrayed you in some small or large way? Ask God for the strength and faith to try and forgive. Or, if you have betrayed a trust that another has put in you, ask God to help you seek forgiveness.

To Help You Reflect
A truthful witness saves lives,
but one who utters lies is a betrayer.
(Prov. 14:25)

Who Says?
Nothing in this world bears the impress of the Son of God so surely as forgiveness.

—Alice Cary, poet

Did You Know?
Forgiveness is not dependent on the person who has wronged you being sorry for her actions.

Notes

SPIRIT BOOSTER #53

What are your favorite Bible verses? Write down a few of them on different index cards and place them in places where you will find them later—in a coat pocket, a drawer, a wallet, and a closet. You'll have fun finding these when you aren't even looking for them!

To Help You Reflect

Happy are those
  who do not follow the advice of the wicked,
or take the path that sinners tread,
  or sit in the seat of scoffers;
but their delight is in the law of the LORD,
  and on his law they meditate day and night.

(Ps. 1:1–2)

Who Says?

The Bible is alive, it speaks to me; it has feet, it runs after me; it has hands, it lays hold on me.

—*Martin Luther, German theologian and reformer*

Did You Know?

The longest verse in the Bible is Esther 8:9, and the shortest is John 11:35.

Notes

SPIRIT BOOSTER #54

Donate a new or gently used Bible to an organization that serves the homeless, abused women, or underprivileged children.

To Help You Reflect

But [Jesus] said to them, "My mother and my brothers are those who hear the word of God and do it."

(Luke 8:21)

Who Says?

Voltaire expected that within fifty years of his lifetime there would not be one Bible in the world. His house is now a distribution center for Bibles in many languages.

—Corrie ten Boom, Dutch Christian
Holocaust survivor, author

Did You Know?

Gideons International, the organization that provides Bibles for hotel rooms, was founded in 1899 in Janesville, Wisconsin.

 Notes

Remember as a child what fun it was to put a bean seed in a wet paper towel and a clear plastic bag, and to watch the roots and plant start to grow? Why not try this experiment again—thinking this time about how your life is rooted in Christ.

To Help You Reflect

As you therefore have received Christ Jesus the Lord, continue to live your lives in him, rooted and built up in him and established in the faith, just as you were taught, abounding in thanksgiving.

(Col. 2:6–7)

Who Says?

It is not my business to think about myself. My business is to think about God. It is for God to think about me.

—Simone Weil, French philosopher

Did You Know?

The roots of a tree grow most from fall through spring.

Notes

SPIRIT BOOSTER #56

Give a small plant to a friend or neighbor with a note attached: "Thank you for helping me find my roots in Christ."

To Help You Reflect

I pray that, according to the riches of his glory, he may grant that you may be strengthened in your inner being with power through his Spirit, and that Christ may dwell in your hearts through faith, as you are being rooted and grounded in love. I pray that you may have the power to comprehend, with all the saints, what is the breadth and length and height and depth, and to know the love of Christ that surpasses knowledge, so that you may be filled with all the fullness of God.

(Eph. 3:16–19)

Who Says?

Never doubt that a small group of thoughtful committed citizens can change the world. Indeed, it is the only thing that ever has.

—Margaret Mead, anthropologist

Did You Know?

Roots on all vegetation have tiny "hairs," and it is these that absorb water and minerals to feed the plant.

Notes

SPIRIT BOOSTER #57

Close your eyes, and feel the warmth of God's face shining upon you, like soft sunlight.

To Help You Reflect

The LORD bless you and keep you;
the LORD make his face to shine
    upon you, and be gracious to you;
the LORD lift up his countenance
    upon you, and give you peace.
                            (Num. 6:24–26)

Who Says?

Far away there in the sunshine are my highest aspirations. I may not reach them, but I can look up and see their beauty, believe in them, and try to follow where they lead.

—Louisa May Alcott, author

Did You Know?

Light travels in straight lines.

Notes

SPIRIT BOOSTER #58

The next time you are out in a crowd or gathering of people, imagine God's face shining softly upon theirs. You may end up seeing people in a different "light."

To Help You Reflect

Again Jesus spoke to them, saying, "I am the light of the world. Whoever follows me will never walk in darkness but will have the light of life."

(John 8:12)

Who Says?

I see heaven's glories shine and faith shines equal.
—*Emily Brontë, British author*

Did You Know?

It takes sunlight approximately eight minutes and twenty seconds to reach the earth.

 Notes

SPIRIT BOOSTER #59

On a card, write, "Blessed am I when _____."
Record your blessings as they happen.

To Help You Reflect

"Blessed are the poor in spirit, for theirs is the king-
dom of heaven.
Blessed are those who mourn, for they will be com-
forted.
Blessed are the meek, for they will inherit the earth.
Blessed are those who hunger and thirst for righ-
teousness, for they will be filled.
Blessed are the merciful, for they will receive mercy.
Blessed are the pure in heart, for they will see God.
Blessed are the peacemakers, for they will be called
children of God."

(Matt. 5:3–9)

Who Says?

In the biblical sense, if you give me your blessing,
you irreversibly convey into my life not just something of the beneficent power and vitality of who you
are, but something also of the life-giving power of
God, in whose name the blessing is given.

—Frederick Buechner, author

Did You Know?

It is the light reflecting from the surfaces of an object that
gives it visibility.

Notes

SPIRIT BOOSTER #60

Jesus sat down and waited for his disciples to sit down and listen to him. Be aware of how well you listen to others. Give the person talking to you your full attention, whether in person or on the phone, and by so doing you will let that person know how important it is for you to listen to what is being said.

To Help You Reflect

"Let anyone with ears to hear listen!"
(Mark 4:9)

Who Says?

Hope begins in the dark, the stubborn hope that if you just show up and try to do the right thing, the dawn will come. You wait and watch and work: you don't give up.

—Anne Lamott, author

Did You Know?

Fish do not have ears with which to hear, but pick up sound vibrations (via pressure changes) through ridges on their bodies.

Notes

SPIRIT BOOSTER #61

Hold your head high! You are wearing a crown of love and mercy. Think of this at times when you need a boost.

To Help You Reflect

Bless the LORD, O my soul,
    and all that is within me,
      bless his holy name.
Bless the LORD, O my soul,
    and do not forget all his benefits—
who forgives all your iniquity,
    who heals all your diseases,
who redeems your life from the Pit,
    who crowns you with steadfast love and mercy,
who satisfies you with good as long as you live
    so that your youth is renewed like the eagle's.
                          (Ps. 103:1–5)

Who Says?

The very contradictions in my life are in some ways signs of God's mercy to me.
        —Thomas Merton, Trappist monk and author

Did You Know?

The bald eagle is the only eagle that is unique to North America.

Notes

SPIRIT BOOSTER #62

If you don't have one already, put up an outdoor bird feeder and know that you are helping to bless God's creation.

To Help You Reflect

"Look at the birds of the air; they neither sow nor reap nor gather into barns, and yet your heavenly Father feeds them."

(Matt. 6:26)

Who Says?

A bird doesn't sing because it has an answer, it sings because it has a song.

—Maya Angelou, poet and author

Did You Know?

The cuckoo bird lays its eggs in the nests of other birds. When the young cuckoo hatches, it pushes the original eggs and fledglings out of the nest and is raised by the foster parents.

Notes

SPIRIT BOOSTER #63

Take a good look at yourself in a mirror. What do you see? You see a person who is a child of God. Remember that when you look at yourself—even in the morning, when your hair is a mess and your eyes are bleary!

To Help You Reflect

But be doers of the word, and not merely hearers who deceive themselves. For if any are hearers of the word and not doers, they are like those who look at themselves in a mirror; for they look at themselves and, on going away, immediately forget what they were like. But those who look into the perfect law, the law of liberty, and persevere, being not hearers who forget but doers who act—they will be blessed in their doing.

(Jas. 1:22–25)

Who Says?

When looking for faults, use a mirror, not a telescope.

—Anonymous

Did You Know?

The Old French word *mirer* means "to look at," while the Latin word *mirari* means "wonder at" (from the Latin *mirus*, which means "wonderful").

◌ Notes ◌

SPIRIT BOOSTER #64

Purchase a small, inexpensive pocket mirror. Give it to someone with a note that says, "When I see you, I think about Christ's love."

To Help You Reflect

For now we see in a mirror, dimly, but then we will see face to face. Now I know only in part; then I will know fully, even as I have been fully known.

(1 Cor. 13:12)

Who Says?

In silence and movement you can show the reflection of people.

—*Marcel Marceau, French mime*

Did You Know?

The island of Murano, off the coast of Italy, is credited with being the place where the first glass mirrors were created in the sixteenth century.

Notes

SPIRIT BOOSTER #65

Substitute time you would normally spend watching a television show and use that time for silence and meditation.

To Help You Reflect

"Now therefore revere the LORD, and serve him in sincerity and in faithfulness. . . . Now if you are unwilling to serve the LORD, choose this day whom you will serve; . . . but as for me and my household, we will serve the LORD."

(Josh. 24:14–15)

Who Says?

God is the friend of silence. See how nature—trees, flowers, grass—grows in silence; see the stars, the moon and the sun, how they move in silence. . . . We need silence to be able to touch souls.

—*Mother Teresa, missionary*

Did You Know?

Although the word "television" was first used in 1900, television broadcasts in the United States weren't available to the general public until 1941.

Notes

SPIRIT BOOSTER #66

Substitute time you would normally spend watching a television show and spend it with a loved one or family member.

To Help You Reflect

Again I saw that under the sun the race is not to the swift, nor the battle to the strong, nor bread to the wise, nor riches to the intelligent, nor favor to the skillful; but time and chance happen to them all.

(Eccl. 9:11)

Who Says?

One always has time enough if one will apply it.

—*Johann Wolfgang von Goethe, German writer*

Did You Know?

According to Nielsen Media Research, the average American watches around one hundred and fifty hours of TV per month.

 **Notes**

SPIRIT BOOSTER #67

Do you wake up early enough to see the sun rise? Try and do that at least once this week, giving thanks for the beauty of the dawning of a new day.

To Help You Reflect
And God saw that the light was good; and God separated the light from the darkness.

(Gen. 1:4)

Who Says?
It is always sunrise somewhere; the dew is never dried all at once; a shower is forever falling; vapor is ever rising. Eternal sunrise, eternal dawn and gloaming, on sea and continents and islands, each in its turn, as the round earth rolls.

—John Muir, naturalist

Did You Know?
A sunrise is not the same as dawn, which is the lightening of the sky before the sun appears.

Notes

SPIRIT BOOSTER #68

Invite someone to watch the sunset with you—even if that person is in another state (you can both agree to watch the sun rise on another day).

To Help You Reflect

A generation goes, and a generation comes, but the earth remains forever. The sun rises and the sun goes down, and hurries to the place where it rises.

(Eccl. 1:4–5)

Who Says?

But beauty seen is never lost,
God's colors all are fast;
The glory of this sunset heaven
Into my soul has passed.
    —John Greenleaf Whittier, poet

Did You Know?

The sun is 300,000 times heavier than the earth.

Notes

SPIRIT BOOSTER #69

Take a walk if you can, and not for exercise, but to enjoy the beauty of God's world.

To Help You Reflect

But as for me, I walk in my integrity;
Redeem me, and be gracious to me.
My foot stands on level ground;
in the great congregation I will bless the LORD.
(Ps. 26:11–12)

Who Says?

The best remedy for those who are afraid, lonely or unhappy is to go outside, somewhere where they can be quiet, alone with the heavens, nature and God. Because only then does one feel that all is as it should be and that God wishes to see people happy, amidst the simple beauty of nature.
—*Anne Frank, Jewish Holocaust victim and author*

Did You Know?

One minute of walking may help extend your life by up to two minutes!

Notes

SPIRIT BOOSTER #70

Tell someone about what you appreciated when you took a walk and took time to appreciate the beauty around you.

To Help You Reflect
Let everything that breathes praise the LORD!
Praise the LORD!

(Ps. 150:6)

Who Says?
I do not at all understand the mystery of grace—only that it meets us where we are but does not leave us where it found us.

—Anne Lamott, author

Did You Know?
On average, a person breathes 22,000 times a day.

--- Notes ---

SPIRIT BOOSTER #71

Try to learn a couple of new words this week, and make them words with a positive meaning.

To Help You Reflect

Show yourself in all respects a model of good works, and in your teaching show integrity, gravity, and sound speech that cannot be censured; then any opponent will be put to shame, having nothing evil to say of us.

(Titus 2:7–8)

Who Says?

Language exerts hidden power, like the moon on the tides.

—Rita Mae Brown, author

Did You Know?

Noah Webster is best known for the dictionaries that bear his name, but in 1833, he also published his own version of the Bible called the "Common Version."

Notes

SPIRIT BOOSTER #72

Be aware of the words you use and the way you use words when you speak to others. A kind word in place of a hurtful one can make a big difference.

To Help You Reflect

Let no evil talk come out of your mouths, but only what is useful for building up, as there is need, so that your words may give grace to those who hear.

(Eph. 4:29)

Who Says?

Kindness is a language which the deaf can hear and the blind can see.

—Mark Twain, humorist and author

Did You Know?

The longest word in the English language that does not contain the vowels *a, e, i, o,* or *u* is "rhythms."

 **Notes**

SPIRIT BOOSTER #73

Begin and end each day with the words "I trust in you, Lord."

To Help You Reflect

Trust in the LORD with all your heart,
   and do not rely on your own insight.
In all your ways acknowledge him,
   and he will make straight your paths.
(Prov. 3:5–6)

Who Says?

To believe in God is for me to feel that there is a God, not a dead one, or a stuffed one, but a living one, who with irresistible force urges us towards more loving.
   —*Vincent van Gogh, Dutch postimpressionist painter*

Did You Know?

According to the developmental psychologist Erik Erikson, basic trust is either learned or not during the first two years of life. Trust is the first learned psychosocial development.

Notes

SPIRIT BOOSTER #74

Do your best to be a person others can trust (even with simple things like being on time).

To Help You Reflect

The LORD is my strength and my shield;
    in him my heart trusts;
so I am helped, and my heart exults,
    and with my song I give thanks to him.

(Ps. 28:7)

Who Says?

Few delights can equal the mere presence of one whom we trust utterly.

—*George MacDonald, Scottish author and clergyman*

Did You Know?

The definition of a legal trust is "a relationship created at the direction of an individual, in which one or more persons hold the individual's property subject to certain duties to use and protect it for the benefit of others." Think of this use of the word "trust" as you ponder putting your trust in God.

Notes

SPIRIT BOOSTER #75

When you begin to feel anxious or worried, take several deep breaths in and out, until you feel calmed.

To Help You Reflect

So do not worry about tomorrow, for tomorrow will bring worries of its own. Today's trouble is enough for today.

(Matt. 6:34)

Who Says?

Worry often gives a small thing a big shadow.

—*Swedish proverb*

Did You Know?

Short-term stress can boost the immune system, but long-term stress suppresses it.

—————— Notes ——————

SPIRIT BOOSTER #76

Be a calming influence. That may be the best gift a person can receive when going through an anxious time.

To Help You Reflect

But I have calmed and quieted my soul,
    like a weaned child with its mother;
    my soul is like the weaned child that is with me.

(Ps. 131:2)

Who Says?

Serenity is not freedom from the storm, but peace amidst the storm.

—Anonymous

Did You Know?

In the eye of the hurricane there is little, if any, precipitation. If happening during the day, a blue sky can be seen; if at night, the stars.

Notes

SPIRIT BOOSTER #77

We carry a reminder of our trust in God every day. Look at a quarter or another coin, and find the words "In God We Trust." When you need a quick reminder to trust in God, pull out a coin.

To Help You Reflect
O Most High, when I am afraid,
    I put my trust in you.
In God, whose word I praise,
    in God I trust; I am not afraid;
    what can flesh do to me?
(Ps. 56:2c–4)

Who Says?
Never be afraid to trust an unknown future to a known God.

Corrie ten Boom, Dutch Christian
Holocaust survivor and author

Did You Know?
"In God We Trust" was first imprinted on a United States coin in 1864 but did not become the official motto of the United States until 1956.

 Notes

SPIRIT BOOSTER #78

Give a coin to a friend and point out that it is a daily reminder in whom we put our trust.

To Help You Reflect

A friend loves at all times,
and kinsfolk are born to share adversity.
(Prov. 17:17)

Who Says?

Basically your friends are not your friends for any particular reason. They are your friends for no particular reason.

—*Frederick Buechner, author*

Did You Know?

The U.S. Mint produced its first coin, a copper cent, in 1793.

Notes

SPIRIT BOOSTER #79

Hold out your palms . . . place in them your trust . . . and hand that trust to God.

To Help You Reflect

But I am not ashamed, for I know the one in whom I have put my trust, and I am sure that he is able to guard until that day what I have entrusted to him.

(2 Tim. 1:12)

Who Says?

Trust the past to God's mercy, the present to God's love, and the future to God's providence.

—Augustine of Hippo, theologian and philosopher

Did You Know?

The word "trust" is both a noun and a verb. As a noun, it is defined by reliance, dependence, and hope. As a verb, it implies the placing of these attributes in someone else's care.

 Notes

SPIRIT BOOSTER #80

By necessity, children must put their trust in others. Often, that trust is abused. Pledge to give time, gifts, or resources to a children's home or children's hospital. If you are not in a position to give, you can always pray.

To Help You Reflect

Give ear, O my people, to my teaching;
    incline your ears to the words of my mouth.
I will open my mouth in a parable;
    I will utter dark sayings from of old,
things that we have heard and known,
    that our ancestors have told us.
We will not hide them from their children;
    we will tell to the coming generation
the glorious deeds of the LORD, and his might,
    and the wonders that he has done.

(Ps. 78:1–4)

Who Says?

The extravagant gesture is the very stuff of creation.

Annie Dillard, author

Did You Know?

The word "mentor," which means "a trusted advisor or guide," comes from Homer's *Odyssey*. Mentor was the name of the trusted friend that was left to watch over Odysseus's home while he was on his travels.

--- Notes ---

SPIRIT BOOSTER #81

Place a small rock or polished stone in a place where you will see it every day, to be a reminder of God as the rock of your salvation. You can even carry the rock in your pocket when you know that you will need an extra dose of strength for the day.

To Help You Reflect

The LORD lives! Blessed be my rock, and exalted be my God, the rock of my salvation.

(2 Sam. 22:47)

Who Says?

Nothing worth doing is completed in our lifetime,
Therefore, we are saved by hope.
Nothing true or beautiful or good makes complete sense in any immediate context of history;
Therefore, we are saved by faith.
Nothing we do, however virtuous, can be accomplished alone.
Therefore, we are saved by love.
No virtuous act is quite a virtuous act from the standpoint of our friend or foe as from our own;
Therefore, we are saved by the final form of love, which is forgiveness.

—Reinhold Niebuhr, theologian

Did You Know?

The words to the hymn "Rock of Ages" were written by Augustus M. Toplady, and first published in Great Britain in 1776 in the journal *Gospel Magazine*.

Notes

SPIRIT BOOSTER #82

Give a small rock or stone to someone else and let them know that the rock is a reminder of God as our rock.

To Help You Reflect

For who is God except the LORD? And who is a rock besides our God?

(Ps. 18:31)

Who Says?

Every block of stone has a statue inside it and it is the task of the sculptor to discover it.
—*Michelangelo Buonarroti, Italian Renaissance artist*

Did You Know?

There are three basic rock types: igneous, sedimentary, and metamorphic, each formed by a very different process. Igneous rocks originate with molten magma, sedimentary rocks from deposits of sediments, and metamorphic from pressure and temperature changes.

Notes

SPIRIT BOOSTER #83

When was the last time you said "thank you" to God, and for what?

To Help You Reflect

On the way to Jerusalem Jesus was going through the region between Samaria and Galilee. As he entered a village, ten lepers approached him. Keeping their distance, they called out, saying, "Jesus, Master, have mercy on us!" When he saw them, he said to them, "Go and show yourselves to the priests." And as they went, they were made clean. Then one of them, when he saw that he was healed, turned back, praising God with a loud voice. He prostrated himself at Jesus' feet and thanked him. And he was a Samaritan. Then Jesus asked, "Were not ten made clean? But the other nine, where are they? Was none of them found to return and give praise to God except this foreigner?" Then he said to him, "Get up and go on your way; your faith has made you well."

(Luke 17:11–19)

Who Says?

Silent gratitude isn't very much to anyone.
—*Gertrude Stein, author*

Did You Know?

Leprosy is now referred to as Hansen's disease, named for the Norwegian physician Gerhard Armauer Hansen, who discovered the bacillus responsible.

Notes

SPIRIT BOOSTER #84

Don't take anyone for granted. Say "thanks!"

To Help You Reflect

And now, our God, we give thanks to you and praise your glorious name.

(1 Chr. 29:13)

Who Says?

If the only prayer you say in your entire life is "Thank you," that would suffice.

—*Meister Eckhart, German theologian and mystic*

Did You Know?

The verb "thank," or "to give thanks," has evolved from the same word for "thought" and "think." Does this imply that offering gratitude is a thoughtful gesture? You decide.

 **Notes**

SPIRIT BOOSTER #85

Rejoice in the gift of this day.

To Help You Reflect

This is the LORD doing;
   it is marvelous in our eyes.
This is the day that the LORD has made;
   let us rejoice and be glad in it.

(Ps. 118:23–24)

Who Says?

True worship from the heart, then, means responding to God's glory and love with our entire being.

—Marjorie Thompson, author

Did You Know?

Psalm 118 was written to accompany the procession of a king and nation into the precincts of the temple following a victory.

 **Notes**

SPIRIT BOOSTER #86

What can you do to make this a good day for someone else? Perhaps rather than *doing* you can focus on *being*. Be the kind of person that reflects the joy of Christ.

To Help You Reflect

Be still, and know that I am God! I am exalted among the nations, I am exalted in the earth.

(Ps. 46:10)

Who Says?

"Don't just do something—stand there!"
— *The White Rabbit, in the Walt Disney animated film version of* Alice in Wonderland *by Lewis Carroll*

Did You Know?

Although there is no scientific proof that it takes more muscles to frown than to smile, it's the meaning behind the idea that counts.

 Notes

SPIRIT BOOSTER #87

This is the word for the week: ASAP—Always Say A Prayer!

To Help You Reflect

Rejoice in the Lord always; again I will say, Rejoice. Let your gentleness be known to everyone. The Lord is near. Do not worry about anything, but in everything by prayer and supplication with thanksgiving let your requests be made known to God. And the peace of God, which surpasses all understanding, will guard your hearts and your minds in Christ Jesus.

(Phil. 4:4–7)

Who Says?

Most of all, Sabbath celebration gives us a deep sense of the Joy that is ours because of the resurrection of Christ, and that festival Joy equips us to glorify God in whatever tasks we might undertake in the following six days.

—Marva Dawn, author

Did You Know?

In the Amplified Bible, the meaning of the word "peace" used in Philippians 4:7 is defined as "that tranquil state of a soul assured of its salvation through Christ, and so fearing nothing from God and being content with its earthly lot of whatever sort that is, that peace."

Notes

SPIRIT BOOSTER #88

Practice gentleness. It is a lost art these days.

To Help You Reflect

Let your gentleness be known to everyone. The Lord is near.

(Phil. 4:5)

Who Says?

Gentleness is the antidote for cruelty.
—*Phaedrus, Roman fabulist*

Did You Know?

The use of the word "gentle" to denote the concepts of "mild" and "tender" was first recorded around 1552, whereas the use of "gentle" as a sense of being "gracious" and "kind" was known much earlier.

 Notes

SPIRIT BOOSTER #89

Add a small branch to your Christmas decorations this year. Place it where you will be reminded of the Bible verses from Jeremiah, and the fulfillment of God's promise in Jesus Christ.

To Help You Reflect

The days are surely coming, says the LORD, when I will fulfill the promise I made to the house of Israel and the house of Judah. In those days and at that time I will cause a righteous Branch to spring up for David; and he shall execute justice and righteousness in the land.

(Jer. 33:14–15)

Who Says?

The great thing about getting older is that you don't lose all the other ages you've been.
—*Madeleine L'Engle, author and Newbery medalist*

Did You Know?

The Spanish explorer Juan Ponce de León is often associated with the idea of a fountain of youth, which he supposedly sought to discover in the New World. While he may have been one of the first Europeans to set foot in what is now the state of Florida, his actually finding of a fountain of youth is legend, and not even an original idea. The quest for a fountain of youth is depicted in many ancient cultures.

Notes

SPIRIT BOOSTER #90

Find out when Hanukkah will be celebrated this year. What are the roots of this holiday, and what does it mean to the Jewish people?

To Help You Reflect

Then Judas and his brothers and all the assembly of Israel determined that every year at that season the days of dedication of the altar should be observed with joy and gladness for eight days, beginning with the twenty-fifth day of the month of Chislev.

(1 Maccabees 4:59)

Who Says?

Kindle the taper like the steadfast star
Ablaze on evening's forehead o'er the earth,
And add each night a lustre till afar
An eightfold splendor shine above thy hearth.

—*Emma Lazarus, poet*

Did You Know?

The name "Hanukkah" is derived from the Hebrew word that means "to dedicate," since the festival celebrates the rededication of the Temple in Jerusalem in the second century BCE.

Notes

SPIRIT BOOSTER #91

What do you imagine that an angel might look like? Where do your concepts come from? Make a sketch of an angel.

To Help You Reflect

And [the angel] came to [Mary] and said, "Greetings, favored one! The Lord is with you." But she was much perplexed by his words and pondered what sort of greeting this might be. The angel said to her, "Do not be afraid, Mary, for you have found favor with God."

(Luke 1:28–30)

Who Says?

We all need to be told that God loves us, and the mystery of the Annunciation reveals an aspect of that love. But it also suggests that our response to this love is critical.

—*Kathleen Norris, author*

Did You Know?

In his 1667 book *The Reasons of the Christian Religion*, English theologian Richard Baxter wrote that "Angels can contract their whole substance into one part of space, and therefore have not partes extra partes. Whereupon it is that the Schoolmen have questioned how many Angels may fit upon the point of a Needle?" (*The Reasons of the Christian Religion* [London: R. White, 1667], 530).

—————— ⟳ **Notes** ⟳ ——————

SPIRIT BOOSTER #92

Visit or call a relative you haven't seen in a long time.

To Help You Reflect

In those days Mary set out and went with haste to a Judean town in the hill country, where she entered the house of Zechariah and greeted Elizabeth.

(Luke 1:39–40)

Who Says?

Nobody has ever before asked the nuclear family to live all by itself in a box the way we do. With no relatives, no support, we've put it in an impossible situation.

—Margaret Mead, anthropologist

Did You Know?

The distance from Nazareth, where Mary lived, and Judea is nearly eighty miles—not a short journey in those days.

 **Notes**

SPIRIT BOOSTER #93

Study some art depicting the visit between Mary and Elizabeth. What do you imagine they thought and felt beyond what the Scripture tells us?

To Help You Reflect

When Elizabeth heard Mary's greeting, the child leaped in her womb. And Elizabeth was filled with the Holy Spirit and exclaimed with a loud cry, "Blessed are you among women, and blessed is the fruit of your womb. And why has this happened to me, that the mother of my Lord comes to me? For as soon as I heard the sound of your greeting, the child in my womb leaped for joy. And blessed is she who believed that there would be a fulfillment of what was spoken to her by the Lord."

(Luke 1:41–45)

Who Says?

When hope is not pinned wriggling onto a shiny image or expectation, it sometimes floats forth and opens.

—*Anne Lamott, author*

Did You Know?

Elizabeth was descended from Aaron, the brother of Moses; so not only Zechariah, but also Elizabeth, came from priestly families.

Notes

SPIRIT BOOSTER #94

Who do you admire as a peacemaker? This can be someone you know, someone famous, or someone you have read or heard about. Why does this person catch your attention?

To Help You Reflect

Those of steadfast mind you keep in peace — in peace because they trust in you. Trust in the LORD forever, for in the LORD GOD you have an everlasting rock.

(Isa. 26:3–4)

Who Says?

It seems to me that there are two great enemies of peace — fear and selfishness.

—Katherine Paterson, author

Did You Know?

The Hebrew word for "peace" is *shalom*, which means "wholeness" or "well-being," in addition to the absence of conflict.

 **Notes**

SPIRIT BOOSTER #95

Recall a favorite Christmas, and a gift you received that was extra special to you.

To Help You Reflect

On entering the house, they saw the child with Mary his mother; and they knelt down and paid him homage. Then, opening their treasure chests, they offered him gifts of gold, frankincense, and myrrh.

(Matt. 2:11)

Who Says?

Faith is different from proof; the latter is human, the former is a Gift from God.

—Blaise Pascal, French mathematician and philosopher

Did You Know?

The word translated as "wise men" in the Matthew account of Jesus' birth (Matt. 2:1) is the Greek word *magi*, which is derived from the same root as the word "magic."

SPIRIT BOOSTER #96

For each gift you receive, donate a new or gently used item to a charity. Or, offer to wrap gifts for someone who is sick, or a family with a new baby, or an older adult who could use the help.

To Help You Reflect

For if the eagerness is there, the gift is acceptable according to what one has—not according to what one does not have. I do not mean that there should be relief for others and pressure on you, but it is a question of a fair balance between your present abundance and their need, so that their abundance may be for your need, in order that there may be a fair balance. As it is written, "The one who had much did not have too much, and the one who had little did not have too little."

(2 Cor. 8:12–15)

Who Says?

I have found that among its other benefits, giving liberates the soul of the giver.

—Maya Angelou, poet and author

Did You Know?

Nearly half of the paper consumed in the United States is gift wrap.

Notes

SPIRIT BOOSTER #97

Keep a running list of the times and ways in which God's presence has filled you with joy.

To Help You Reflect

May the God of hope fill you with all joy and peace in believing, so that you may abound in hope by the power of the Holy Spirit.

(Rom. 15:13)

Who Says?

Happiness is attached to happenings, but joy is not attached to happenings. Joy is attached to God.
— *The Rev. Dr. Vashti McKenzie, first female bishop in the African Methodist Episcopal Church*

Did You Know?

Symphony no. 9 in D Minor, op. 125 (*Choral*), turned out to be Beethoven's final symphony. The words sung to the final movement are adapted from Friedrich Schiller's poem "Ode to Joy." Beethoven's Ninth marked the first time that a major composer used voices in a symphony.

 Notes

Design a cornerstone that you would use if you built your own house. What significant dates or events would you inscribe on this stone? If you own your home, consider painting a cornerstone with this information.

To Help You Reflect

So then you are no longer strangers and aliens, but you are citizens with the saints and also members of the household of God, built upon the foundation of the apostles and prophets, with Christ Jesus himself as the cornerstone. In him the whole structure is joined together and grows into a holy temple in the Lord; in whom you also are built together spiritually into a dwelling place for God.

(Eph. 2:19–22)

Who Says?

I simply can't build my hopes on a foundation of confusion, misery, and death.

—*Anne Frank, Jewish Holocaust victim and author*

Did You Know?

In architecture, a cornerstone is a stone where two intersecting walls meet. A cornerstone is sometimes inscribed with the date of a building's completion, or with some other information of historical importance.

Notes

SPIRIT BOOSTER #99

Make a small time capsule using a jar or even a plastic-coated envelope. On individual pieces of paper, write down your ten favorite Bible verses. Leave the time capsule in your home, in an attic, under a floor tile (when you're replacing that old floor), inside a wall (during a renovation—no need to break a hole in the wall). Choose a place where the time capsule can be discovered one day after you no longer reside in that home, as a kind of legacy of your life.

To Help You Reflect

The effect of righteousness will be peace, and the result of righteousness, quietness and trust forever.

(Isa. 32:17)

Who Says?

Forever—is composed of Nows.

—Emily Dickinson, poet

Did You Know?

English mathematician John Wallis (1616–1703) is often credited with creating the symbol used for infinity (∞). Wallis served as a cryptographer in Parliament and is also recognized as one of the founders of modern calculus.

————— ∽ **Notes** ∾ —————

SPIRIT BOOSTER #100

How will you leave the world a better place for your having been a grateful inhabitant of this earth? Remember, it need not be any great accomplishment. Creating a home where all are welcome, smiling at strangers, and collecting for a worthy charity are examples of what you may have done, or plan to do. Ponder the ways in which your life gives glory and honor to God.

To Help You Reflect

You are worthy, our Lord and God, to receive glory and honor and power, for you created all things, and by your will they existed and were created.

(Rev. 4:11)

Who Says?

Christians should never fail to sense the operation of an angelic glory. It forever eclipses the world of demonic powers, as the sun does a candle's light.

—*Beverly Sills, operatic soprano*

Did You Know?

The word "glory" is one of the most common words in the English Bible. "Glory" may refer to a physical manifestation, an attribute of God, and a faithful response to the divine.

Notes

QUOTED SOURCES

The number in parentheses indicates the number of the Spirit Booster where this person is quoted.

Aesop (6)
Alcott, Louisa May (57)
Angelou, Maya (62) (96)
Anonymous (3) (20) (63) (76)
Arendt, Hannah (49)
Aristotle (40)
Augustine (5) (17) (79)
Bacon, Francis (32)
Barclay, William (23)
Bennett, Arnold (18)
Brontë, Emily (58)
Brown, Rita Mae (71)
Browning, Elizabeth Barrett (1)
Buechner, Frederick (29) (59) (78)
Buonarroti, Michelangelo (82)
Carroll, Lewis (86)
Cary, Alice (52)
Charnock, Stephen (47)
Clemens, Samuel Langhorne. *See* Twain, Mark
Coffin, William Sloane, Jr. (10) (14)
Confucius (37)

Daly, Mary (50)
Dawn, Marva (87)
Dickinson, Emily (99)
Dillard, Annie (80)
Donne, John (27)
Eckhart, Meister (84)
Fosdick, Harry Emerson (15) (34)
Frank, Anne (69) (98)
Gandhi, Mahatma (41)
Goethe, Johann Wolfgang von (66)
Greenwood, Lee (21)
Hanh, Thich Nhat (7)
Henry, Matthew (36)
Holiday, Billie (31)
Holmes, Oliver Wendell (43)
Judge, Thomas A. (12)
Kierkegaard, Søren (28)
King, Martin Luther, Jr. (39)
Lamott, Anne (60) (70) (93)
Lazarus, Emma (90)
L'Engle, Madeleine (89)
Lewis, C. S. (24)
Luther, Martin (53)

MacDonald, George (11)
(74)
Marceau, Marcel (64)
McKenzie, Vashti (97)
Mead, Margaret (56) (92)
Merton, Thomas (61)
Moody, Dwight L. (44)
Mother Teresa (2) (65)
Muir, John (67)
Newman, John Henry (30)
Niebuhr, Reinhold (81)
Norris, Kathleen (38) (51)
(91)
Northrup, Christiane (46)
Pascal, Blaise (95)
Paterson, Katherine (94)
Phaedrus (88)
Reed, Myrtle (8)
Sandburg, Carl (25)

Schweitzer, Albert (9)
Sills, Beverly (100)
Stein, Gertrude (83)
ten Boom, Corrie (54) (77)
Thomas à Kempis (19)
Thompson, Dorothy (16)
Thompson, Marjorie (45)
(85)
Tillich, Paul (13)
Twain, Mark (72)
van Gogh, Vincent (73)
Vaughn, Ruth (33)
Weil, Simone (26) (55)
Wharton, Edith Newbold
(4)
Whitman, Walt (35)
Whittier, John Greenleaf
(68)
Wordsworth, William (42)

SCRIPTURE REFERENCES

*The number in parentheses indicates the number of the Spirit
Booster where this Scripture is quoted.*

Old Testament

Genesis 1:1–2 (41)
Genesis 1:4 (67)
Genesis 1:31–2:3 (1)
Numbers 6:24–26 (57)
Deuteronomy 15:7 (12)
Deuteronomy 28:3–6 (45)
Joshua 24:14–15 (65)
Ruth 1:16–17 (49)
1 Samuel 12:24 (34)
2 Samuel 22:47 (81)
1 Chronicles 29:13 (84)
Psalm 1:1–2 (53)
Psalm 1:3 (42)
Psalm 18:31 (82)
Psalm 26:11–12 (69)
Psalm 27:1 (16)
Psalm 27:14 (26)
Psalm 28:7 (74)
Psalm 34:4–8 (29)
Psalm 46:10 (86)
Psalm 51:10–12 (5)
Psalm 56:2c–4 (77)
Psalm 61:4 (22)
Psalm 63:1–4 (44)
Psalm 71:1–5 (40)
Psalm 78:1–4 (80)

Psalm 86:1–6 (13)
Psalm 86:7 (14)
Psalm 91:11–12 (21)
Psalm 103:1–5 (61)
Psalm 118:23–24 (85)
Psalm 119:105 (17)
Psalm 131:2 (76)
Psalm 139:1–6 (37)
Psalm 150:6 (70)
Proverbs 3:5–6 (73)
Proverbs 6:20–23a
   (18)
Proverbs 14:25 (52)
Proverbs 17:17 (78)
Proverbs 27:4 (47)
Ecclesiastes 1:4–5 (68)
Ecclesiastes 9:11 (66)
Isaiah 26:3–4 (94)
Isaiah 32:17 (99)
Isaiah 40:28–31 (25)
Jeremiah 31:33–34 (33)
Jeremiah 33:14–15 (89)
Micah 6:8 (8)
Wisdom of Solomon
   7:21–23 (32)
1 Maccabees 4:59 (90)

New Testament

Matthew 2:11 (95)
Matthew 4:1–2 (19)
Matthew 4:11 (20)
Matthew 5:3–9 (59)
Matthew 5:9 (36)
Matthew 6:26 (62)
Matthew 6:34 (75)
Matthew 7:1–5 (38)
Matthew 17:2–8 (27)
Matthew 17:5 (28)
Mark 4:9 (60)
Mark 12:28–31 (11)
Mark 14:17–19, 29–31 (51)
Luke 1:28–30 (91)
Luke 1:39–40 (92)
Luke 1:41–45 (93)
Luke 1:78–79 (35)
Luke 6:38 (10)
Luke 8:21 (54)
Luke 17:11–19 (83)
John 1:1–5 (4)
John 8:12 (58)
John 14:25–27 (43)
John 14:27 (36)
John 20:22 (7)
Romans 12:2 (30)

Romans 15:13 (97)
1 Corinthians 12:4 (3)
1 Corinthians 12:11 (31)
1 Corinthians 13:12 (64)
2 Corinthians 5:17–19 (6)
2 Corinthians 8:12–15 (96)
Galatians 5:25–26 (48)
Ephesians 2:19–22 (98)
Ephesians 3:16–19 (56)
Ephesians 4:29 (72)
Philippians 4:4–7 (87)
Philippians 4:5 (88)
Colossians 2:6–7 (55)
Colossians 3:12 (9)
1 Thessalonians 1:2–3 (46)
2 Timothy 1:12 (79)
Titus 2:7–8 (71)
Titus 3:15 (2)
Hebrews 1:1–3 (50)
Hebrews 4:15 (19)
Hebrews 11:1 (39)
Hebrews 13:2 (20)
James 1:12 (23)
James 1:13 (24)
James 1:22–25 (63)
1 John 4:16–18 (15)
Revelation 4:11 (100)